To [Ira?], in honor of Shane Stone and share of words; it is a rare and precious thing. Much happiness. Terri L. French

A Ladybug on My Words

Terri L. French

illustrated by
Logan Tanner

Copyright © 2010 by Terri L. French.

All rights reserved.

For Ray, who has taught me to appreciate life's moments.

writing outdoors
a lady bug punctuates
my words

plastic begonias
in the flower box--
one frustrated bee

watering the daisies
trying not
to sprinkle the spider

focusing
on a butterfly...
leaf photo

shoe-tying. . .
the carpenter ant
detours

my wine glass
half empty--
wishing on fireflies

echo in the pines
the hoot owl tires
of answering

on the trail--
does the chickadee
hear the sparrow?

wishing on the first star
for the last time--
mockingbird's song

dove on the phone line   calling

one note

of the warbler's song--

this moment

catching tadpoles--
this summer he wades
d
e
e
p
e
r

meandering. . .
even daydreams
follow the river's bend

gentle rain--
the chant of Spring peepers
joins my zen

shouldering the weight
of the oil spill--
pelican wings

in her palm
an olive shell--
pull of the tides

beach reading--
the sandcrab's eyes and mine
meet

sheets hung to dry
tonight
smelling sunshine

wind
blowing on the child
blowing on the pinwheel

storm warning
the rustle of branches
one tree to another

before the thunder
my bones
know

slipping by
the weathervane--
still winds

the first dandelion. . .
welcome

just a hearth
and a line of daffodils--
home

planting herbs
pausing
just to breathe

hot summer night
the 4 o'clock's petals
still closed

napping to Vivaldi
the air-conditioner
hums

raised
to the desert sun--
saguaro arms

lighting the tiki torches
he thinks of
an old flame

early moon--
she pats blue corn masa
into perfect circles

closing my eyes
to feel moss--
braille trail markers

after the rain
the curls in her hair
tighter

a spot of blood
on the unfinished quilt--
harvest moon

glancing at my wrist
for the first time
mountain shadows

Made in the USA
Charleston, SC
10 June 2013